THEMATIC UNIT
POPCORN

Written by Janet Hale

Illustrated by Sue Fullam and Keith Vasconcelles

Teacher Created Materials, Inc.
P.O. Box 1040
Huntington Beach, CA 92647
©*1992 Teacher Created Materials, Inc.*
Made in U.S.A.

ISBN 1-55734-263-6

Table of Contents

Introduction

Popcorn is a poppin' perfect thematic unit to utilize during the fall season (October is National Popcorn Month)... or any time of the year! Its 80 pop-ular pages are filled with a wide variety of lesson ideas, activities, and activity sheets designed for use with primary students. At its core are three high-quality children's literature selections, *Popcorn, The Popcorn Book*, and *The Popcorn Dragon*. For each of these books, activities are included which set the stage for reading, encourage the enjoyment of the book, and extend the concepts gained. In addition, the theme is connected to the curriculum with lessons in language arts, math, science, social studies, art, music, and life skills (cooking, physical education, etc.). Many of these activities encourage cooperative learning. Suggestions and patterns for bulletin boards and unit management tools are additional time savers for the busy teacher. Furthermore, directions for student-created books, Big Books, and culminating activities allow students to synthesize their knowledge in order to produce products that can be shared beyond the classroom. These directions highlight this very complete teacher resource.

This thematic unit includes:

literature selections—summaries of three children's books with related lessons (complete with reproducible pages) that cross the curriculum

poetry—suggested selections and lessons enabling students to write and publish their own works

planning guides—suggestions for sequencing lessons each day of the unit

language experience ideas—daily suggestions as well as activities across the curriculum, including Big Books

bulletin board ideas—suggestions and plans for student-created and/or interactive bulletin boards

homework suggestions—extending the unit to the child's home

curriculum connections—in language arts, math, science, social studies, art, music, and life skills such as cooking, physical education, and career awareness

group projects—to foster cooperative learning

a culminating activity—which requires students to synthesize the learning to produce a product or engage in an activity that can be shared with others

a bibliography—suggested additional literature and nonfiction books on the theme

---

To keep this valuable resource intact so that it can be used year after year, you may wish to punch holes in the pages and store them in a three-ring binder.

Introduction (cont.)

Why Whole Language?

A whole language approach involves children in using all modes of communication: reading, writing, listening, observing, illustrating, experiencing, and doing. Communication skills are interconnected and integrated into lessons that emphasize the whole of language rather than isolating its parts. The lessons revolve around selected literature. Reading is not taught as a separate subject from writing and spelling, for example. A child reads, writes (spelling appropriately at his/her level), speaks, listens, etc. in response to a literature experience introduced by the teacher. In this way, language skills grow naturally, stimulated by involvement and interest in the topic at hand.

Why Thematic Planning?

One very useful tool for implementing an integrated whole language program is thematic planning. By choosing a theme with correlating literature selections for a unit of study, a teacher can plan activities throughout the day that lead to a cohesive, in-depth study of the topic. Students will be practicing and applying their skills in meaningful contexts. Consequently, they will tend to learn and retain more. Both teachers and students will be freed from a day that is broken into unrelated segments of isolated drill and practice.

Why Cooperative Learning?

Besides academic skills and content, students need to learn social skills. No longer can this area of development be taken for granted. Students must learn to work cooperatively in groups in order to function well in modern society. Group activities should be a regular part of school life and teachers should consciously include social objectives as well as academic objectives in their planning. For example, a group working together to write a report may need to select a leader. The teacher should make clear to the students and monitor the qualities of good leader-follower group interaction just as he/she would state and monitor the academic goals of the project.

Why Big Books?

An excellent cooperative whole language activity is the production of Big Books. Groups of students, or the whole class, can apply their language skills, content knowledge, and creativity to produce a Big Book that can become a part of the classroom library to be read and reread. These books make excellent culminating projects for sharing beyond the classroom with parents, librarians, other classes, etc. Big Books can be produced in many ways and this thematic unit includes directions for at least one method you may choose.

Popcorn

by Frank Asch

Summary

Sam Bear's parents go to a costume party. What will Sam do? Have a party of his own! Little did he know everyone would choose to bring the same yummy treat—popcorn. Cooperatively, the guests pop popcorn until it fills up the house, literally! Still working together they eat up the puffy flakes before Sam's parents return. Later, Mama and Papa Bear return with a present for him...oh, my, what could it be?

Note: Before beginning unit, carefully prepare the bulletin board on page 61. Read Watch Your Language, Please! (pages 67-74) to gain an accurate knowledge of popcorn. The outline below, and on pages 14-15 and 24, are sequential suggested plans for using the various activities in this unit. You may wish to adapt them to fit your classroom needs.

Sample Plan

Day I	Day II
• Popcorn Pass-Arounds (# 1, page 6)	• Share Day I Homework
• Pop Popcorn (# 2, page 6)	• Poppin' Good Graphing (page 43)
• Read *Popcorn* book (#1, page 7)	• That's A Quote! Quotation Marks (page 40)
• A Popcorn Twist (# 2, page 7)	• Make Bear Masks (page 52)
• The 1-Cup Mystery (#1, page 8)	• A Quotation Popcorn Play (Re-enacting the story, # 2, page 9)
• Pop + Corn = Compound Words! (page 39)	• Utilize Popcorn Story Starters (page 33)
• Homework: Send Home Bear-y Essential Note (page 57)	• Homework: Students Create Popcorn Pictures (page 52)
• Prepare Popcorn Treats to serve on Day II. (page 55)	

Overview of Activities

Setting the Stage

1. To spark interest in your theme, create teams of four students and provide each team with one Popcorn Pass-Around sheet (page 11). Students take turns passing the sheet around and drawing a picture and/or writing words pertaining to the subject of popcorn. Discuss completed sheets!

2. Pop popcorn with your students. Children love to watch and listen to the popcorn kernels in action! Discuss how popcorn flakes look, feel, and smell while placing individual servings into small cups, bowls, or plastic bags. Allow students to munch away while listening to the *Popcorn* book.

3. Begin, rather than end, the unit with a field trip to a farm which grows and processes corn plants. Students will return to the classroom with plenty of questions which can be written on chart paper (using a black marker). Display chart. As students discover answers to their questions, write answers using a contrasting marker color. (This makes a great evaluation alternative to paper-pencil testing.)

Overview of Activities *(cont.)*

Enjoying the Book

1. Have students sit close around you with their containers of popcorn. Study the book cover together. Ask predictable answer-type questions so that students "discover" what season it is (Fall). Ask why they think the book is entitled *Popcorn*; share responses. Read the story straight through, until the third-to-last page. Have students predict what the present could be; verbalize or list on chart paper, then complete story reading.

2. Create an innovation. Instead of having the guests bringing popcorn, students work cooperatively to come up with a different food or non-food item, new characters or character names, and possibly a new twist to what kind of problem(s) the food/items will cause. When the class has decided on the elements, brainstorm text and write it out onto large, sturdy chart paper. Allow students to pair up and each illustrate a page. Bind pages together to create a class Big Book (page 34).

3. Pass out 12" x 18" pieces of white construction paper to each student. Students divide paper into three sections and label sections: Beginning, Middle, Ending (for younger students, pre-write the words). Discuss/review the meaning of each word. Students illustrate events from the story in appropriate sections. Display on bulletin board, or in hallway area for all to see! (An alternative: Use the wheel book pattern (page 35) and direct students to use the first section to illustrate the cover page and the three remaining sections for illustrating the three parts of the story.)

Overview of Activities *(cont.)*

"Oh, no! Not again!"

4. At the end of the story, we really don't know what Sam Bear's reaction was to his gift. Present the lesson on quotation marks (page 40). Finish by having students individually think of a new "last page." Each student writes out the extra text using quotation marks and illustrates it on a large popcorn pattern (page 66). Staple the pages together (before stapling, see Creating Class Books, page 36). Add covers entitled "Popcorn Possibilities!"

5. Using Sam Bear pattern (pages 12-13), have students create a new costume for Sam or decorate him with the costume they plan to wear for their fall or Halloween activities. If possible, allow students to use multi-mediums, such as fabrics, paints, colored chalk, and sequins to decorate their bears.

Extending the Book

1. Sam and his friends did not realize that just a small amount of popcorn kernels create a lot of popcorn flakes. Place one cup of popcorn kernels in front of the class. How many kernels are in one cup? Allow students to estimate... then share that the answer is approximately 1,600 kernels! (If you have time, verify by counting kernels using a 1's, 2's, 5's, or 10's pattern.) Ask students to predict how many cups of popcorn flakes will be made from one cup of unpopped kernels. Now pop and see! Usually, one cup unpopped equals 24 popped cups. (The popped flakes, as well as the old maids, can be used for other popcorn activities in this unit.)

1 CUP

Overview of Activities *(cont.)*

2. Create a re-telling of the story by presenting a Popcorn Play utilizing quotation mark sentence strips to reinforce the learning. The play is designed for a team of ten students. You may wish to form two separate "play" teams, using extra students for set designers, directors, quote coaches, or producers. After practices and a dress rehearsal, the Popcorn Play can be presented to another class or video-recorded to be shown during "A Poppin' Good Performance" (Culminating Activity, page 59). Copy the story's quoted text (see chart below and next page) onto sturdy sentence strips. When a student is saying his/her lines, have him/her simultaneously hold up the appropriate quoted sentence strip. Remember, the objective is for students to visualize, as well as hear, the connection between quotation marks and the spoken words.

Note: It is helpful to use a different colored sentence strip for each character's text.

The book *Popcorn* is not numbered. To follow the page numbers given on the chart, start numbering with one where the story text begins.

Character	Quoted Text
Sam Bear	"Wear a costume and bring something good to eat." "What happened?" "No, you've got to stay and help me get rid of all this popcorn, or I'll be in big trouble." "Munch, munch." "What is it?"

Overview of Activities (cont.)

Popcorn Play Parts (cont.)

CHARACTER	QUOTED TEXT
Mama and Papa Bear (Make 2 sets)	"Take good care of the house and we'll bring you a present." "Wake up." "We brought you a present." "Popcorn!"
Betty Bear	"I brought some popcorn for the party." "Hey, let's pop all that popcorn." "Who turned out the lights?" "Crunch, crunch." "I feel like my stomach is going to burst."
Buster Bear	"Where did everybody go?" "Munch, munch." "I don't care if I ever see another piece of popcorn in my whole life."
Bobby Bear	"Help. Get me out of here!" "Gulp." "Mine, too."
Narrator Bear 1	Reads/Memorizes text on pages one through seven, including such phrases as, ". . . she said," on page four.
Narrator Bear 2	Reads/Memorizes text on pages nine through seventeen, including phrases.
Narrator Bear 3	Reads/Memorizes text on pages nineteen through twenty-seven, including phrases.
Narrator Bear 4	Reads/Memorizes text on pages twenty-eight through thirty-six, including phrases.

Popcorn Pass-Around

See directions on page 6.

Team Names

_____   _____

_____   _____

Sam Bear Pattern

Tab A

Sam Bear Pattern *(cont.)*

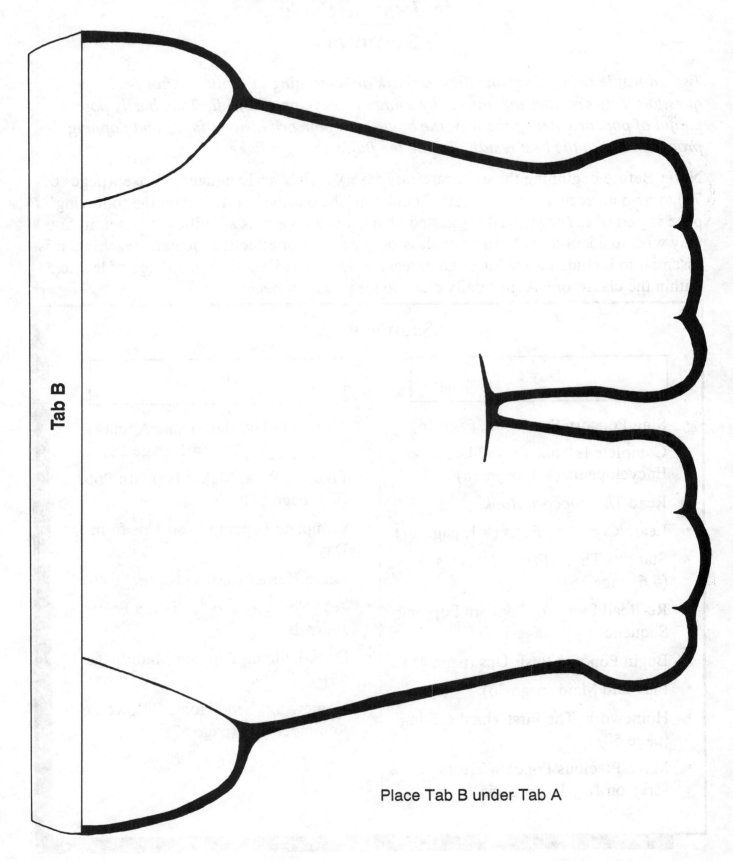

Tab B

Place Tab B under Tab A

The Popcorn Book

by Tomie dePaola

Summary

Two adorable twins, Tony and Tiny, embark on a learning adventure. After posing a question, Tiny provides the answer by using an encyclopedia while Tony busily pops a panful of popcorn. Along the way, the boys learn popcorn history, facts, and popping procedures with the best result... eating the fluffy popcorn flakes!

Note: Before beginning the unit, carefully read Watch Your Language, Please! (pages 67-74) to gain an accurate knowledge of popcorn. The outline below and on the following page is part of the sequential suggested plan for using various activities in this unit. You may wish to adapt them to fit your classroom needs. For effective thematic teaching, it is essential to include re-teaching and extensive time to address the wide range of learners within the classroom. Adjust daily plans to meet learner needs.

Sample Plan

Day I	Day II
• Sing Popcorn Songs (#1, page 16)	• Complete The Best Thing About _____ Is... (# 1, page 18)
• Complete Is That a Fact? Use of an Encyclopedia (# 3, page 16)	• Find out What Makes Popcorn Pop? (# 3, page 17)
• Read *The Popcorn Book*	• Complete Popcorn Push-Ups from Day I
• Learn Corn-Fed Facts (# 1, page 17)	• Learn Kernel Knowledge (page 46)
• Start "Is That a Fact!" Journals (# 6, page 18)	• Add New Facts to "Is That a Fact!" Journals
• Re-Read Story for Popcorn Popping Sequence (# 2, page 17)	• Do A-maizing Popcorn Math (page 43)
• Begin Popcorn Push-Ups (page 45)	• Homework: Send Home Pillowcase Reminder Slip (page 57)
• Play Old Maid (page 56)	
• Homework: The First Thanksgiving (page 50)	
• Make Precious Popcorn Treats to serve on Day II. (page 55)	

Sample Plan *(cont.)*

Day III

- Recite Popcorn Poetry (# 2, page 16)
- Make Popcorn Pillowcase Poems (page 42)
- Learn Through a Salty Experience! (# 4, page 18)
- Write Bear-y Important Letters (# 5, page 18)
- Practice Popcorn Place Value (page 44)
- Learn About Corn-y People (# 3, page 19)
- Add New Facts to "Is That a Fact!" Journals
- Homework: Take Home Memorization Slip (page 58) and Pillowcase Poem

Day IV

- Re-read *The Popcorn Book*. List Native American information on chart paper and discuss
- Read Native American Tribes Map (page 49)
- Have a Popcorn Throwing Contest (page 44)
- Make Popcorn Soup (page 55)
- Do (Make) Popcorn Soup Predictions and Graphing   (# 2, page 19)
- Create A Corn Growing Cycle Fold-Out Book (# 4, page 20)
- Make Popcorn Necklaces (page 53)

Day V

- Meet The Author Tomie dePaola (page 23)
- Read Other Books by Mr. dePaola; Compare and Contrast Illustrations/ Text (Bibliography, page 80)
- Create "Our Popcorn Book" and Mail to Mr. dePaola (# 5, page 20)
- Write "A Poppin' Good Performance" Invitations (page 59 and 75)
- Review Using Popcorn Review Cards (page 77-78)

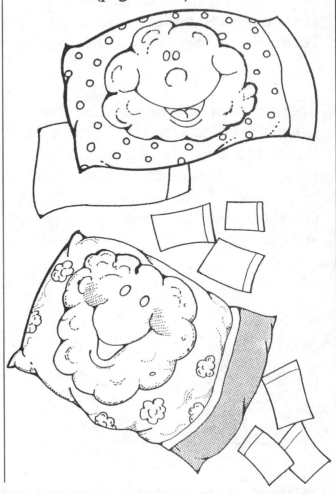

Overview of Activities

Setting the Stage

1. Use one or more of the songs on page 54 to create a joyful atmosphere for the learning to come. When teaching the song(s), have the words written out on chart paper so students can see the speech-written print connection. When students are comfortable with the words and tune, try singing the song(s) in round-robin or echo form!

2. Share the poems (page 32, written out on chart paper), asking students to identify skills presently being taught/reviewed (for example: rhyming words; beginning/ending sounds; vowels; vowel variants). Keep poems on display for the Popcorn Pillowcase Poem activity (page 42) and free-reading time.

3. Research is an essential learning strategy. Young students, as well as older ones, need to be aware of this learning concept. Show the class a volume "P" encyclopedia. Ask if anyone knows what the book is and how it is used. Explain that it helps people find facts (true pieces of information) about people, places, and things. Share that a "P" encyclopedia is used in the story *The Popcorn Book*. Ask them to pay close attention to what question the encyclopedia helps the boys answer, and be ready to share at the end of the story.

4. Draw a popcorn kernel on a piece of chart paper. Have students brainstorm and predict how old the oldest popcorn kernels (seeds) ever found were. List predictions on the chart. Share that *The Popcorn Book* will tell them the answer. When you are finished reading the book, ask them to tell you the answer and compare it to their predictions; discuss.

Overview of Activities *(cont.)*

Enjoying the Book

1. Often times adults, as well as children, do not know the difference between popcorn and other corn. To better comprehend and synthesize the concept of popcorn, students need to be aware of the various corn varieties. Use the Types of Corn information (pages 67-68) as a springboard to this learning. Use the Corn-y Worksheet (page 21), or have students draw their own pictures to reinforce the learning. Display worksheets or student drawings!

2. First, re-read *The Popcorn Book* to obtain the sequence of how to pop popcorn; list Tony's steps on chart paper. Next, have students brainstorm safety tips needed when making popcorn. (Permission from parent(s); have clean utensils and supplies ready; be careful around a hot stove; use a pot holder to remove lid from hot pot; clean up when finished cooking.) Last, have students (individually or in teams) generate their own Popcorn Procedure Guides to popping popcorn using enlarged large popcorn patterns (page 66); display.

3. Looking back through the story, re-read the page stating that Native Americans of long ago thought popcorn popped because an angry little demon lived inside each kernel. This kind of a story is called a myth or legend. Share that you want them to pretend that they do not know why popcorn pops and write their own legend. Reproduce page 22 on 8 ½" x 11" white paper and pass out one copy to each student. Go over directions and let students begin. When they are finished, share the myths and display them in the library for all to read and enjoy.

Overview of Activities *(cont.)*

4. A Salty Experience. Share that last night, before you went to bed, you read both the *Popcorn* story and *The Popcorn Book* and you noticed something very interesting! Ask them to listen carefully... (Page 21 of *The Popcorn Book*) "But if salt is put in the pan **before** the kernels are popped, it makes the popcorn tough." (Page 12 of *Popcorn*) "He added some oil and **salt** and turned on the stove." Hmmm, who is correct? Conduct a taste-testing experiment to find out! Follow the directions on page 47 and take a vote!

5. After completing #4 above, write a letter to Sam Bear using the Sam Bear Pattern (pages 12-13) to tell him he made his popcorn correctly/incorrectly. Display letters with a Salty Experience explanation.

6. There is a wealth of information and facts in *The Popcorn Book*. Have each student write about their new knowledge in an "Is That a Fact!" journal. Create journals by reproducing the large blank popcorn pattern (page 66) so each student has a five to ten page journal, including a cover page. Students will add new facts each day for the remainder of the Popcorn thematic unit. The student-created books can then be used as an evaluation tool for the testing of student mastery in writing, punctuation, language, and/or science facts.

Extending the Book

1. Have Precious Popcorn Treats (page 55) cut and ready. Ask what Tony and Tiny said was the best thing about popcorn. (Eating it!) Share that you think the best thing about popcorn is... making Precious Popcorn Treats (show treats). Pass treats out and let everyone enjoy a tasty tasting experience. While eating, ask students to think of a word that could replace "popcorn" in the sentence, "The best thing about _____ is..." and complete the sentence ending. Have each student write out an innovative sentence and illustrate it using a large popcorn pattern (page 66). When everyone is done, ask students to stand in a large circle (facing the center) and take turns "popping" the popcorn patterns up into the air, reciting their sentences and showing the illustrations.

Overview of Activities *(cont.)*

2. As a class, make Native American Popcorn Soup (page 55). While it is simmering, have students predict if they will like/not like the taste of the soup. Write the predictions on an enlarged popcorn pattern (page 66) divided into two labeled sections; display. After tasting the soup, have students complete a second graph. Compare results.

3. On pages 73 and 74, you will find people who have influenced the world of popcorn. Divide the class into research teams (teams can be headed by a higher grade level student, parent volunteer, or classroom aide). Each team will be responsible for presenting an oral report on a corn-y person. Provide encyclopedias and/or other informational resources for the research projects. Inform teams that they may choose from a variety of oral presentation options such as: poster, VCR tape, song, play, or bulletin board display.

Overview of Activities *(cont.)*

4. Using additional resources, share the Native American corn growing cycle and discuss the sequential pattern. (An excellent resource is Aliki's *Corn Is Maize*! Bibliography, page 80.) Have students create Fold-Out Books (directions, page 36) to show comprehension of the corn-growing process.

5. Create an "Our Popcorn Book" for Tomie dePaola. Using the large popcorn pattern (page 66), have each student write a separate letter to Mr. dePaola. If possible, glue a school picture of each child onto his/her letter page. Create "extra" pages by gluing photographs of the class participating in some of the Popcorn unit activities. Students can help write explanatory sentences under the photos. Staple pages together, add a cover and mail this extra-special gift to Mr. dePaola (address, page 23).

6. Have students brainstorm other uses for popcorn besides "eating it"! Make, do, or explore some of the ideas, activities, or projects generated.

20

Corn-y Worksheet

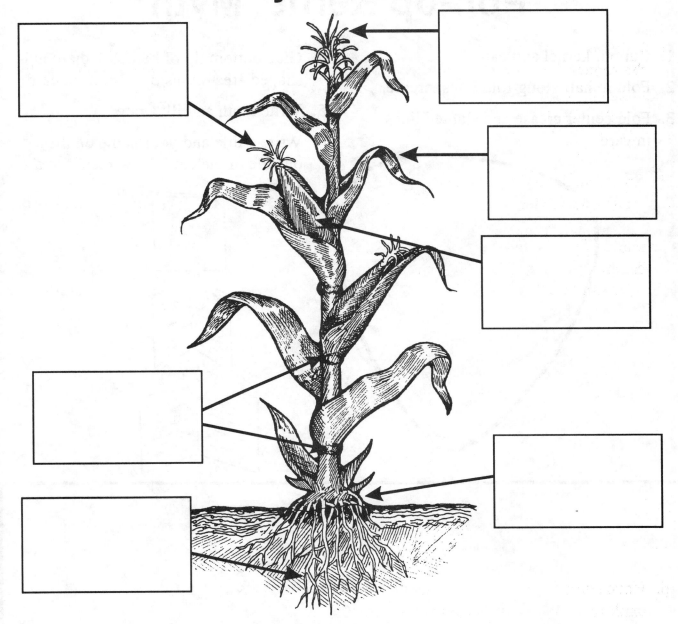

Directions: Cut out the labels and glue into the correct boxes.

tassel	nodes	prop roots	silk
stalk	leaves	ear and husk	roots

Teacher Note: Answers on page 69. For a challenge, have students alphabetize words.

Pop-up Kernel Myth

1. Cut out kernel and card.

2. Fold in half along fold lines; crease.

3. Fold center crease and slanted lines inward.

4. Glue bottom tip of kernel in diamond-shaped area on inside of opened card.

5. Write myth and illustrate.

6. Write a title and your name on the outside of the card. Now read it to a friend.

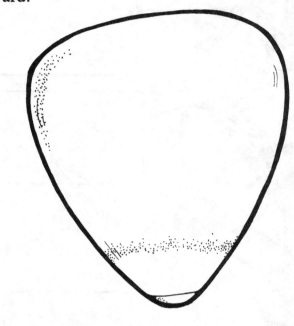

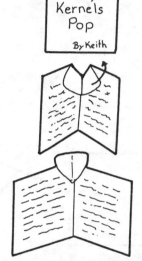

Meet the Author

Students (and adults) love to learn more about the personal side of an author and illustrator. It makes a book seem "alive," because a "real" person wrote it! Below you will find information about Tomie dePaola, which can be shared with your class.

Tomie dePaola is a famous author and artist. He has written and/or illustrated nearly 200 books.

Born on September 15, 1934 in Meriden, Connecticut, Tomie now lives in New Hampshire with his three Welsh terriers, Madison, Morgan, and Moffat, and his three cats, Foshay, Dayton, and Bomba. He works in his studio which is a huge barn that is over 100 years old.

Tomie's ideas come "from most anywhere and everywhere." He says "...I got the idea to write *The Popcorn Book* while I was eating a big bowl of popcorn!"

He started drawing as a little boy with a special pencil his grandfather gave him. In high school he took art classes and after graduation he "practiced, and practiced and practiced."

When Tomie signs his name he always draws a heart inside the T in Tomie. This shows his love for life, children, and the world around him.

Tomie dePaola

Send letters to:

Tomie dePaola
G.P. Putnam's Sons - 11th Floor
200 Madison Avenue
New York, NY 10016

The Popcorn Dragon

by Jane Thayer

Summary

Dexter discovers that he can blow smoke and begins to show off. He wants to have friends, but his antics cause the giraffe, zebra, and elephant to walk away. Saddened, he lies down in a popcorn field and is awakened by the delicious smell...of popcorn! He learns an important lesson in life—to have friends, first you must be one!

Note: Before beginning the unit, carefully read Watch Your Language Please! (pages 67-74) to gain accurate popcorn knowledge. The outline below is part of the sequential suggested plan for using the various activities in this unit. You may wish to adapt them to fit your classroom needs.

Sample Plan

Day I

- "Show Off" Dragon Thought Web (# 1, page 25)
- Read *The Popcorn Dragon*
- Re-tell story with Stick Puppets (# 1, page 25)
- Complete *The Popcorn Dragon* Story Web (page 31)
- Make a Dragon Sponge Painting (page 53)
- Compare Seeds (# 2, page 26)
- Make a Pop-Open Dragon Book (#1, page 26)
- Homework: Send home Be A Poppin' Good Friend Coupons (page 76)

Day II

- Create Story Book Jacket (page 34)
- Create a "Let's Be Polite Popcorn Field" (# 3, page 26)
- Review and rehearse your choice for "A Poppin' Good Performance" Activities (page 59)
- Play Popcorn Relay Race (page 56)
- Homework: Send home/bring back Popcorn Pillowcase Poem Slip (page 58)

Day III

- Culminating Activities
- Evaluation
- A Poppin' Good Performance (page 59)

Overview of Activities

Setting the Stage

1. Dexter is a show-off. Make a copy of Dexter (page 28) and glue him on the corner of a piece of chart paper along with the question, "Are You a Show-Off ?" Have students brainstorm what a show-off is and what a show-off does to get attention. List responses on the chart paper.

2. Create one set of story stick puppets to help introduce the characters and setting of the story. Reproduce the cut-out figures on pages 28-30 and glue them onto craft sticks.

3. Show the cover of *The Popcorn Dragon*. Ask students to look carefully at the illustration. Is there any popcorn in the picture? Promote critical thinking by asking the question, "Why do you think this story has the title *The Popcorn Dragon* when there is no popcorn in the picture?" List responses, then read the story. Afterwards, have students create a new cover on 9" x 12" white construction paper, this time including popcorn (which reflects part of the story's text). Share and display.

Enjoying the Book

1. Have each student (or pair of students) create one set of story stick puppets (page 28-30). Re-read the story together. Each time a specific character is speaking, have the students hold up the appropriate stick puppet. When re-reading is completed, extend the learning by having the students use the stick puppets to re-tell the story to one another, students from another room, the principal/school staff, and/or parents!

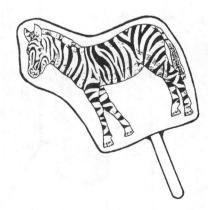

Overview of Activities *(cont.)*

2. Animals do not get to eat freshly popped popcorn in the wild! But they do get to eat seed-bearing fruits and vegetables. Have students create patterns, weigh, and make "adjective" observations about different sizes, shapes, and kinds of seeds.

3. Students should have learned about the parts of a cornstalk during a previous lesson (#1, page 17). Have students work in teams of three or four to draw a large cornstalk on butcher paper and cut out. Provide each student with a small popcorn pattern (page 66) and have everyone write a sentence which explains one way they, or someone else, can be polite. (Students may want to brainstorm while working on the cornstalks.) Display cornstalks loaded with polite popcorn sentences in the hallway. Complete display by adding the title "A Poppin' Polite Corn Field."

Extending the Book

1. Following the Pop-Open Book directions on page 37, have students create a Pop-Open Dragon Book. The character can be Dexter or an innovation. The objective of the Pop-Open Dragon Book is to share ways in which we can be good friends, and to practice the use of quotation marks (page 40). After putting books together, allow students to read them to each other. Display the Pop-Open Dragon Books in your library where everyone can read how to be the best friend they can be!

Overview of Activities *(cont.)*

2. List the adjectives that are used to describe Dexter (green scaly body; long twisty tail; short knobby knees; bat-like wings; hot breath). Use this as a springboard into a new or review lesson on adjectives (or describing words). Make a class chart and post so students can refer to it as they write!

Adjectives = *Describing Words*
green scaly long knobby

3. Most books have a dedication page. Discuss the purpose and meaning of a dedication page. Read examples from various authors, but focus on Jane Thayer's dedication, "To the Cooks, who knew Dexter first." Ask students to brainstorm what Jane Thayer's dedication means. Explain that as a part of their next writing activity, they will need to dedicate their story (book) to someone. Have students write out to whom they will dedicate their next story (and why) on index cards. Keep this handy for the next writing experience.

4. Since *The Popcorn Dragon* is about friendship you may wish to expand upon this idea. Let your class try some cooperative activities such as add-on stories in which you give a team of three or four students a story with a beginning. The team takes turns writing one line each and passing it to the next person in the group. Start the story with the line "Once there was a group of friends who liked popcorn. They all..." Or let students write acrostic poems based on the friends in *The Popcorn Dragon*. As a group do one about Dexter. As an extension let children write them about their own friends.

D arling Dragon
E xciting and
X -traordinary
T ried to get
E verything
R ight when popping corn

For more ideas about the friendship theme refer to TCM 274 Thematic Unit-Friendship and TCM 280-Friends.

Story Stick Puppets

*See page 25 for suggested uses.

Dexter

Mother Dragon

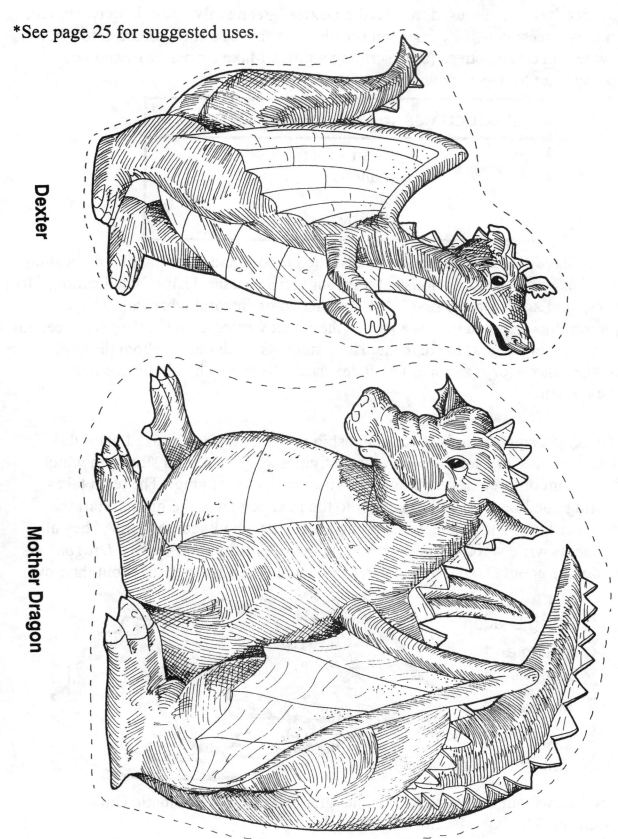

28

Story Stick Puppets *(cont.)*

*See page 25 for suggested uses.

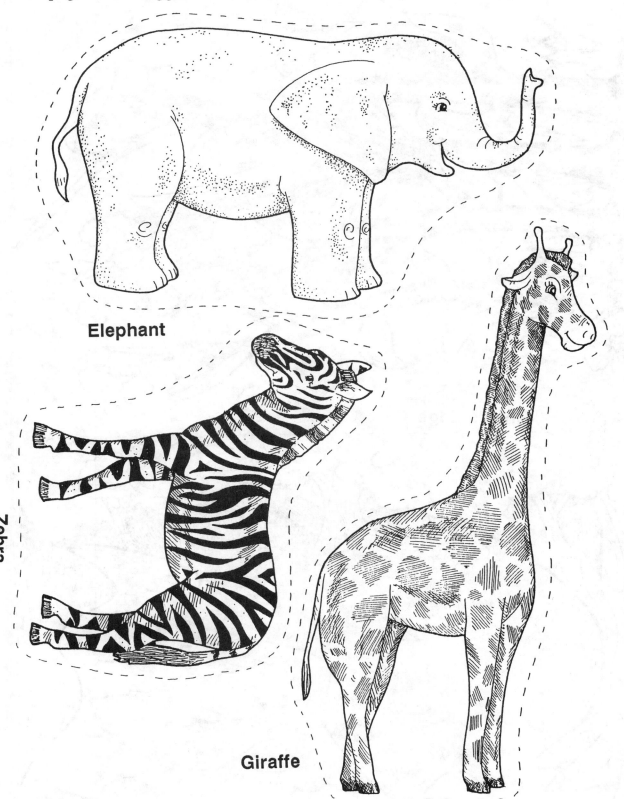

Elephant

Zebra

Giraffe

Story Stick Puppets (cont.)

*See page 25 for suggested uses.

Popcorn Field

River's Edge

30

Name _____

The Popcorn Dragon Story Web

Cut out the ovals. Paste them in correct places to make a story web.

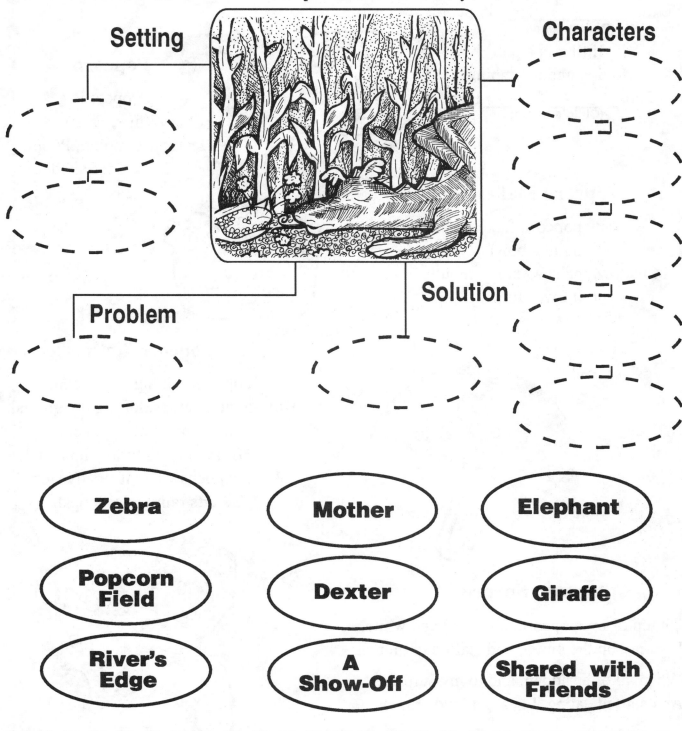

Setting

Characters

Problem

Solution

Zebra

Mother

Elephant

Popcorn Field

Dexter

Giraffe

River's Edge

A Show-Off

Shared with Friends

- -

(Fold under before reproducing)

Answers:
Setting: River's Edge; Popcorn Field
Problem: A Show-Off

Solution: Shared with Friends
Characters: Dexter; Mother; Elephant; Giraffe; Zebra

Popcorn Poetry

Pop, Pop, Pop!

Little _____ Popcorn,
(Child's Name)
    Sitting in a pot.
   Moving and a jumping,
Pop, _____ Pop!
(Child's Name)

Popcorn

Popcorn
White, Fluffy
Heating, Jumping, Popping
Buttered, Salted
Tasty!

Popcorn Flakes

I saw popcorn flakes
Sitting in a bowl.
"Munch-Munch" went my mouth,
until I was full!

Popcorn Rain

Popcorn raining all around,
Hitting the treetops, hitting the ground.
Hitting my umbrella here,
Hitting my umbrella there.
What happens when it finally stops?
It starts raining lollipops!

Popcorn Surprise

On top of my popcorn, all fluffy and white,
I poured on the butter, and started to munch.

When all of a sudden, and to my surprise,
As I started eating, I heard a loud crunch.

So I checked my loose tooth, and guess what I found,
Not only was it missing, it must have gone straight down!

*Teacher Note: Students can create their own poetry for the Popcorn Pillowcase Poems.

Popcorn Story Starters

Reproduce as many starters as needed. Cut out and place starters in a popcorn sack or cup. Let each student draw a starter and begin to write!

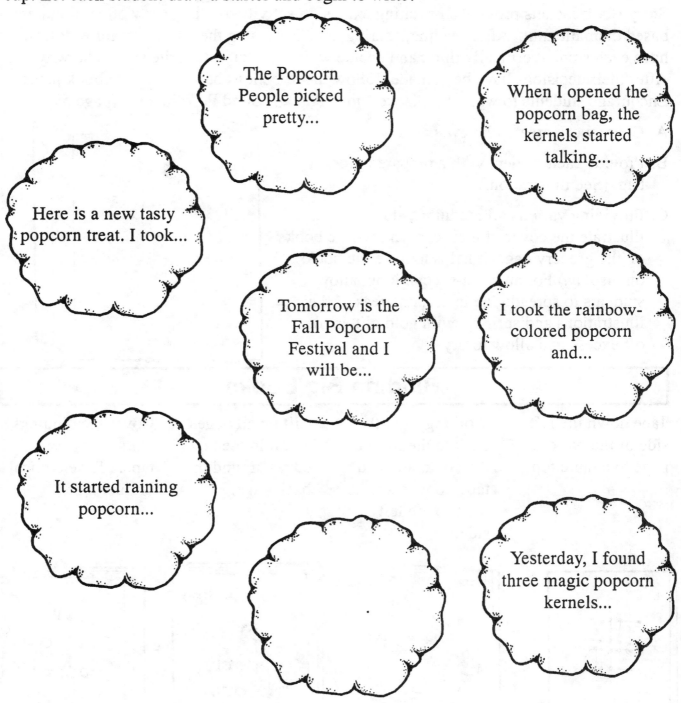

The Popcorn People picked pretty...

When I opened the popcorn bag, the kernels started talking...

Here is a new tasty popcorn treat. I took...

Tomorrow is the Fall Popcorn Festival and I will be...

I took the rainbow-colored popcorn and...

It started raining popcorn...

Yesterday, I found three magic popcorn kernels...

Use the blank so you can write in your own story starters.

Creative Book Directions

Story Book Jackets

Story Book Jackets provide an exciting extension activity to this, or any other, literature-based thematic unit. After reading, sharing, and discussing the unit's literature stories, have each student critically think and decide which was their favorite story, and why. After their decisions have been made, follow the directions below to create book jackets. Encourage students to wear their jackets to A Poppin' Good Performance (page 59).

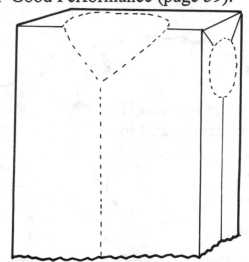

A. Cover work area with newspaper.

B. Provide each student with a prepared grocery bag. (See illustration.)

C. Providing various art mediums, students illustrate the cover of their chosen favorite book on the grocery bag. (It helps to have the books on display.) For an extra-special look, allow students to spread glue in certain areas of their illustrations and sprinkle with gold glitter. Tap off excess and allow to dry.

Binding Big Books

Tape down the left side of the back page to a table top.

Working from the back to the front of the book, add and tape down each page to the left side.

Lift up all pages and fold the tape edges around the back page.

Cover the bindings with strong, wide tape. (Try electrical or duct tape.)

Creative Book Directions *(cont.)*

Wheel Books

Each student will need a cover wheel (pattern below) and a separate identically-sized white circle sheet which, when divided into four parts, will have sections to match the size of the window on the pattern. When all sections have been illustrated, the student writes the title of the concept/story/poem and his/her name on the cover wheel. Assemble the wheel book by placing a paper fastener through the centers of the two wheels. Be sure that the back sheet can turn easily.

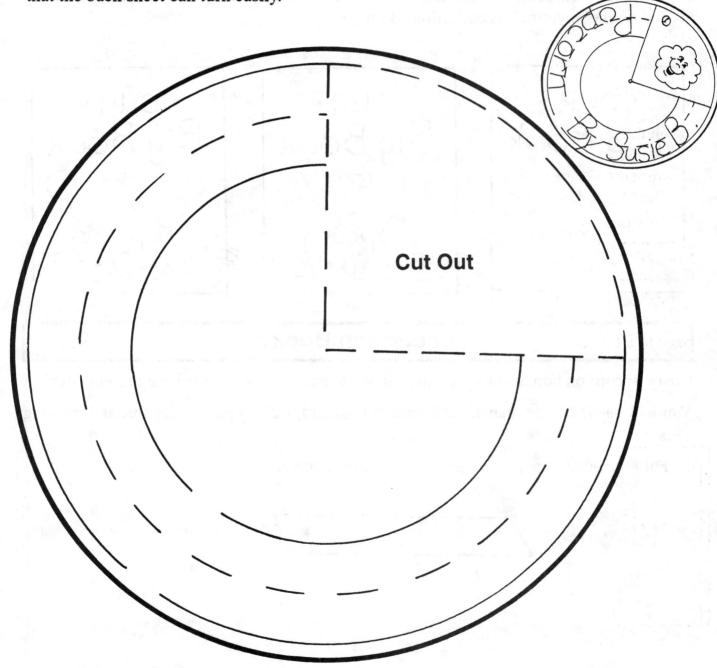

Cut Out

Creative Book Directions *(cont.)*

Creating Class Books

When creating a class library of student-authored books, it often seems like it takes forever! Here is a little trick to triple your collection. When you are writing a class story book that is not sequential (in other words, each page is independent from the other), you can take the total number of pages and divide them into three books of equal or near-equal pages (for example: Divide 30 pages from 30 students into 3 books of 10 pages each). Cover each book with the same cover and instantly you have added three books instead of one to your class collection. Hooray!

Accordion Books

Create accordion books to sequentially illustrate and write about the corn growing cycle.

You will need: butcher paper, cardboard or tagboard, writing paper, crayons, and marking pens.

1. Fold the butcher paper in half lengthwise for strength.

Creative Book Directions *(cont.)*

Accordion Books *(cont.)*

2. Divide the paper into 8 sections.

3. Insert a piece of tagboard or cardboard into each end to make the book stand up easily. Tape the ends together.

4. Put sentences and illustrations on separate sheets of paper. Glue the pages to each section of the accordion book.

5. Use the popcorn pattern on page 66 and glue it on the front as a cover.

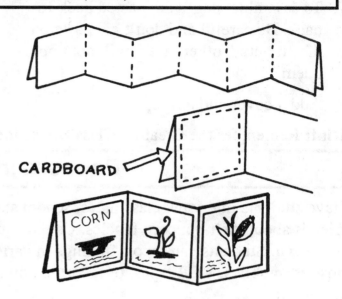

CARDBOARD

Pop-Open Books

Pop-open books are a "mouthful" of fun! Follow the basic directions below to create a pop-open blank page.

1. Fold an 8 ½" x 11" piece of paper in half lengthwise; crease.

2. Cut a 1" slit on fold line at halfway point on folded paper.

3. Diagonally fold Areas A and B; crease.

4. Open paper and reverse folds by poking them to the inside.

5. Close and re-press. Open to make sure "beak" (pop-open section) is opening correctly.

6. Draw animal and write appropriate text.

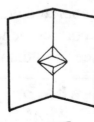

Creative Book Directions (cont.)

Pop-Open Books (cont.)

7. To assemble, pages are pasted back-to-back. Be careful and don't get paste on the "mouth," otherwise it will not pop open!

8. Add a cover and a title.

Hint: Remember the Creating Class Books idea on page 36.

Popcorn Interviews

Have students interview classmates, school staff, family members, or neighborhood friends about their popcorn fancies. Use the questions below, or have students generate their own. Students can report findings in various ways such as oral/written reports, posters, mobiles, VCR tapes, or recording on audio-cassettes.

Do you like popcorn?
When do you like to eat popcorn?
Where do you like to eat popcorn?
With whom do you like to eat popcorn?
What is your favorite way to make popcorn?
What is your favorite flavor/brand of popcorn? Why?
Do you know how big the biggest popcorn ball ever made was? (It was 4' 5" tall and weighed 450 lbs.!)

Poppin' Good Sentences

Create a chart (shown below) using the colored small popcorn pattern (page 65). Have students brainstorm words and/or phrases for each column. Next have students create poppin' good sentences (using generated words/phrases) by writing the words with corresponding colored markers, colored pencils, or crayons to visually conceptualize the sentence structure. Share sentences and display.

	describing word	who or what	did what	where	when
A The An	green fuzzy old	bear plant bug	crawled slept grew	in the park by a river in a window	today this week in the winter

Compound Words

*"Compound words are two words
put together to make one word."*

A perfect time to introduce or reinforce the concept of compound words is during a pop + corn unit! Follow the outline below, or implement your lesson plan.

1. Show various pictures of compound words (i.e. butterfly, raincoat, snowflake, pancakes, firefly, doghouse, football). Have students name the pictures.

2. Write the compound words on the chalkboard. Ask if they notice anything interesting about these words. Some may notice "little words" in the "big words." If not, help them "discover" by circling the two words with different colors of chalk.

3. Say statement above, along with hand movements. Have students repeat with hand movements. Practice until concept is understood.

4. Provide additional compound word examples, or allow students to brainstorm their own, and create compound popcorn pictures. Provide one large and two small popcorn patterns (pages 65 and 66) and have students write and illustrate a compound word.

"That's a Quote!"

" When you pop me, I become a popcorn flake."

Quotation marks tell us who is talking.

Quotation marks can seem very abstract to young learners. Follow the outline below to help students understand this concept.

1. Make a statement; repeat it. Write the statement on the chalkboard including quotation marks.

"I like to teach," said Mrs. Fish.

2. Repeat the process with an additional two or three sentences. Ask students if they noticed anything "funny" or "different" about the sentences you wrote on the board. Some may notice the "little lines" you placed at both ends of the sentence. If they do not, circle the quotation marks with a different color of chalk.

3. Share that the "little lines" are quotation marks and they tell us who is talking. Relate this back to what you said/wrote.

4. Ask a few students to provide a sentence. Write exactly what was said on the board. Include quotation marks.

5. Pass out books that contain quotation marks. Have student pairs/teams locate quotation mark sentences in the books; discuss. Complete worksheet (page 41) together or individually.

6. Have students work in pairs (or, if younger students, with teacher/parent aide or older student) and write quotation mark sentences of their own; display.

"That's a Quote!" Worksheet

Cut and paste the sentences that tell us someone is talking.

"I can read."

That is a dog.

"Can you help me?"

"What is that?"

"My name is Sam."

Find the ball.

Take two now.

"I love you!"

See the cat.

Popcorn Pillowcase Poems

Follow the directions below to create an excellent "across the curriculum" experience combining reading, writing, listening, memorizing, art, and family participation.

Begin by:

1. Sending home the reminder slip (page 57) asking students to bring in clean, non-printed pillowcases.

2. Introducing poems as suggested for #2, page 16.

3. Sharing the project objective: Students will memorize a poem and recite it orally to the class.

4. Having each student choose the poem he/she wishes to learn. Students may want to write and learn their own poem.

To Create a Popcorn Pillowcase Poem:

A. Place a double-folded piece of butcher paper in between the two sides of the pillowcase. (This will prevent ink from bleeding through the fabric.)

B. Have students trace out what they want to draw and write with a pencil.

C. Use permanent markers or acrylic paint mixed equally with textile medium (available at most craft stores) to write the poem and color drawings on the pillow case.

D. Allow to dry, remove the butcher paper and send home with reminder slip on page 58 so that memorizing can begin.

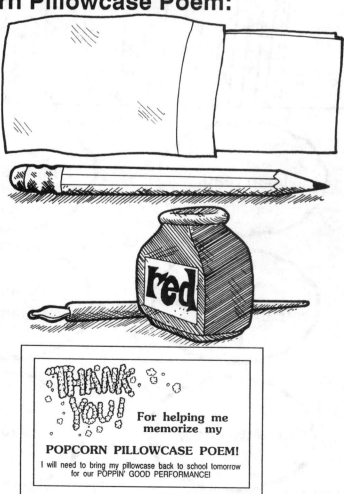

THANK YOU!

For helping me memorize my

POPCORN PILLOWCASE POEM!

I will need to bring my pillowcase back to school tomorrow for our POPPIN' GOOD PERFORMANCE!

Poppin' Good Math

Popcorn Graphing

Provide pairs or teams of students with small bowls of colored popcorn kernels (available in most grocery stores). Have students sort kernels by color and create a color/number graph. Have students color the graph in with the matching color.

Number	red	blue	green	yellow	orange
8	░				░
7	░				░
6	░				
5	░		░		░
4	░		░		░
3	░	░	░	░	░
2	░	░	░	░	░
1	░	░	░	░	░

Have students compare/contrast the differences on their own and other teams' graphs using mathematical terminology. Example: "We had a greater number of red kernels than Sally and Joey."

A-Maizing Popcorn Math

Long ago, when Native American tribes roamed the Americas, parents taught their children how to add and subtract using common items such as popcorn kernels and/or popcorn flakes. Allow students to practice their math concepts utilizing this age-old method.

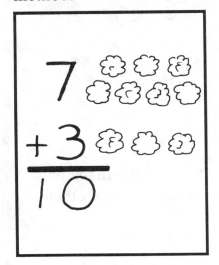
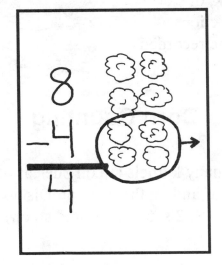

Poppin' Good Math *(cont.)*

Popcorn Place Value

As stated on the previous page, Native American tribes of long ago taught their children math using common items. Why not use popcorn kernels and flakes to teach place value concept? Here are some examples:

To test double-digit place value mastery, provide each student with a sheet of tagboard containing five numerals along the left side. Student then glues down popcorn flakes (for tens) and kernels (for ones).

Popcorn Throwing Contest

During an evening around the campfire, young braves often threw popcorn kernels directly into the fire and tried to catch them as the flakes popped out! Since this might not be too safe to do at school, have each student predict how far they can throw a popcorn flake. Have everyone throw from a designated line on the floor. Measure the distances with a ruler, yardstick, or measuring tape. Were the predictions correct? Discuss and display the recorded popcorn throwing distances.

Corn Counting

Ask students to estimate how many kernels are on one ear of multi-colored, ornamental corn. Provide teams with one ear and let them count. Discuss results and methods they used for counting (counting by 1's, 2's, 5's, 10's, and so on).

Name _____

Popcorn Push-Ups

Hypothesis

Can popcorn kernels "push" a lid off of a jar?

YES   NO
(Circle one.)

Prepare

Fill a baby food jar with popcorn kernels. Add water up to the rim of the jar. Place a small square piece of aluminum foil over the top of the jar. Allow kernels to sit overnight.

Prediction

With a red crayon, circle what you think will happen or use a red crayon to write your own prediction.

1. Kernels will look the same tomorrow.

2. Kernels will be smaller tomorrow.

3. Kernels will be bigger tomorrow.

4. _____

Draw your jar here.

YES   NO
(Circle one.)

Result (To be completed on second day.)

Draw a picture of what your jar of kernels looks like now.

What happened to the kernels? Circle the answer under the **prediction** section with a blue crayon.

Were your prediction and result the same?

Write what you have learned on the back of this experiment sheet.

Draw your jar here.

A Popcorn Kernel

Cut out the labels on the bottom of the page and glue them in the correct boxes.

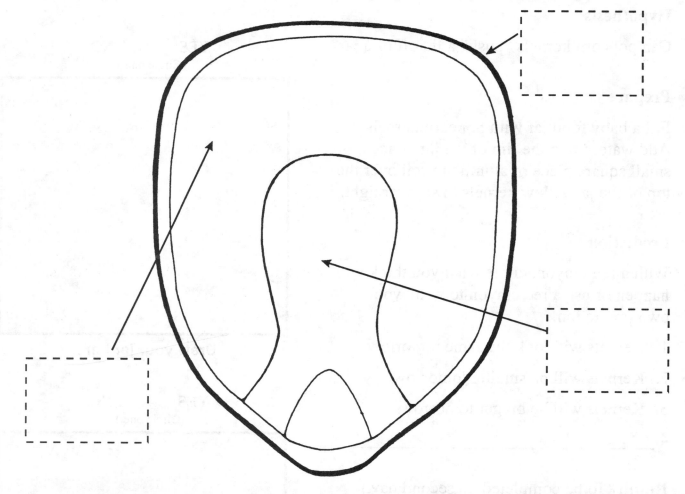

endosperm or food	seed coat or hull	embryo or baby plant

Teacher Note: Allow students to observe cut open water-soaked kernels used in the Popcorn Push-Up activity (page 45). Cover key before copying.

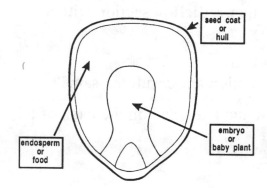

Popcorn Experiments

A Salty Experiment

Conduct a taste-testing experiment to see if salt added to the oil before popping popcorn kernels makes the flakes less tasty than when the salt is added to the popcorn flakes after popping (see # 4, page 18). Prepare popcorn flakes utilizing both "salting methods." Place the two popped popcorn flakes in separate bowls behind a screen. Each student sits in front of the screen and is provided a small paper cupful of both types of popcorn, but is not told which is which. After tasting both types, the student states which popcorn type tasted the best; record/tally answer. After everyone has tasted (don't forget the teacher needs to taste-test, too!), place the tally results on a bar graph and discuss results.

Which Pops the Most?

There are a variety of ways to pop popcorn. The most pop-ular are metal pot on stove with oil, hot air popper, and standard popper. Which method pops the most popcorn flakes? Conduct an experiment. Begin by having students predict which method will produce the most popped flakes, and why. Write prediction statements on chart paper. For each method:

1. Count out 400 kernels (approximately ¹/₄ cup).

2. Pop as method requires.

Popcorn Experiments *(cont.)*

3. Count number of popped flakes and old maids. Draw results utilizing a circle graph format.

Sample Graphs:

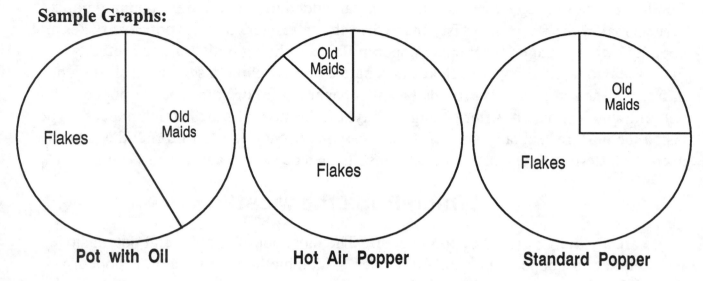

Pot with Oil   Hot Air Popper   Standard Popper

4. Compare the three method results to the prediction statements and discuss. Display charts and new conclusion statements in the hallway to share with everyone.

How Kernel That Be?

If you drop popcorn kernels in water, they sink. If you drop popcorn flakes in water, they float. Why? Have students predict.

Share that this is because the puffed flakes are less dense (not as compact) as kernels. This means that the flakes are "lighter" than the water so they float, while the kernels are "heavier" than the water and sink. Share that, even though this is true, you can make kernels float! Follow directions below and show the class.

1. Fill a glass with soda water. Place a few popcorn kernels in the glass.

2. After a few moments, the kernels will begin to rise to the surface, then go back down, only to rise up again. Let the students hypothesize "why" they are floating, then share how you conducted the experiment.

The phenomena happens because soda water contains a gaseous element, and the "gas" is attracted to the kernels. When enough gas bubbles form around the kernel, it "lifts" it to the surface. The gas is then released into the air and the kernel sinks back down.

Native American Tribes Map Reading

Use the map key to fill in the blanks.

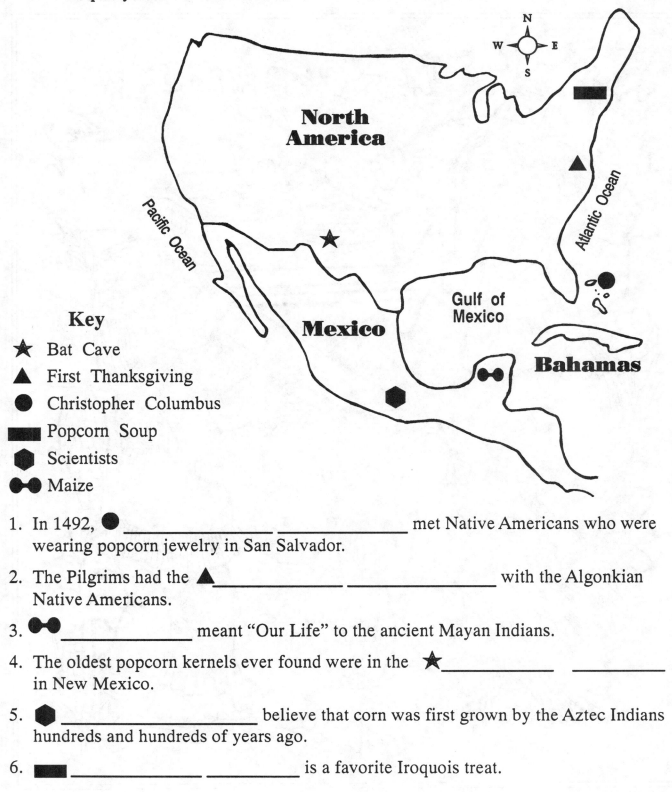

1. In 1492, ● _____ _____ met Native Americans who were wearing popcorn jewelry in San Salvador.

2. The Pilgrims had the ▲_____ _____ with the Algonkian Native Americans.

3. ●●_____ meant "Our Life" to the ancient Mayan Indians.

4. The oldest popcorn kernels ever found were in the ★_____ _____ in New Mexico.

5. ⬡_____ believe that corn was first grown by the Aztec Indians hundreds and hundreds of years ago.

6. ▬_____ _____ is a favorite Iroquois treat.

The First Thanksgiving

Popcorn was given to the Pilgrims as a gift during the first Thanksgiving Feast by a Native American named Quadequina. Can you find the hidden 15 popcorn flakes?

A Popcorn Business

Set up a "free enterprise" system, with your students as the business managers. Sell bags of popcorn in the lunch room or after school and use the earnings for classroom supplies, field trips, or helping to fund a needy cause.

Students will have to decide:

1. "Company" Management
2. Price of Popcorn
3. Set-up and Clean-up Procedures
4. Quality Control
5. Use(s) of Profits

Happy Selling!

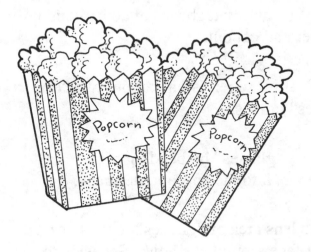

Bear Masks

Bear Masks can be used as costume "props" for the Quotation Popcorn Play.
(See # 2, page 9.)

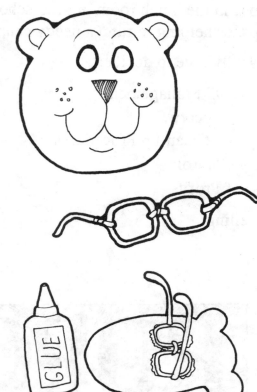

1. Students draw free-hand pictures of bear faces on sturdy tagboard or construction paper and cut out.

2. With adult supervision, cut out two "eye holes" in mask.

3. Create "glasses" by bending pipe cleaners into the appropriate shape.

4. Glue lens area of "glasses" to the back of bear face around eye holes. Set aside to dry.

5. Student wears bear mask like a regular pair of glasses.

Popcorn Pictures

Have students create a design or picture using popcorn seeds, popcorn flakes, or both. Background paper will need to be sturdy, tagboard works well. Students use crayons or paint to create main drawing features, then glue on popcorn pieces on for a special 3-D effect! Display popcorn pictures for all to see.

52

Popcorn Necklace

Popcorn necklaces are created in the same way as cranberry garlands. Provide each student with a strong cotton thread (approximately 20 inches long), needle (for younger students, pre-thread the needles), and popcorn flakes. Tie off the two ends of the thread when necklace is long enough to go over student's head.

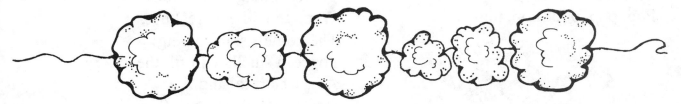

Dragon Sponge Painting

Students will have fun and reinforce geometrical shape concepts while creating Dexter or another dragon friend.

1. Cover work area with newspaper.

2. Place tempera paints in shallow bowls (number of colors determined by teacher).

3. Lay out one set of a pre-cut square, circle, triangle, and rectangle sponge for each color available.

4. Students dip sponges into paint and onto provided 12" x 18" white paper to create a dragon picture.

5. Allow to dry; display. (Note: If you wish to add the dragons to "A Poppin' Polite Corn Field" see # 3, page 26.)

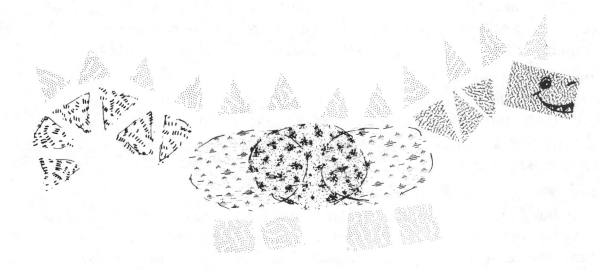

Popcorn Songs

The Popcorn Song
(To the tune of "Frère Jacques")
See the popcorn, see the popcorn.
Popping up, popping up.
Very tasty eating,
Very tasty eating,
Pop, pop, pop! Pop, pop, pop!

Sing a Song Of Popcorn
(To the tune of "Sing a Song of Sixpence")
Sing a song of popcorn,
A mouthful full of fun!
Four-and-twenty kernels,
There's going to be a ton!
When the oil gets real hot,
The kernels start to ping!
Popcorn smells will fill the air,
As we start to sing...
(Start song over again!)

Pop-Tee-Pop
(To the tune and basic movements of "Looby Loo")
To begin, students are standing in a circle:

1. Here we go Pop-Tee-Pop,   *(Hop in a circle to the right.)*
   Here we go Pop-Tee-Tee.   *(Hop in a circle to the left.)*
   Here we go Pop-Tee-Pop,   *(Hop back to the right.)*
   Now look at me!   *(Hop back to the left.)*
   I put my salt shaker in,   *(Hand extended toward center.)*
   I put my salt shaker out.   *(Hand pulled away from center.)*
   I give my salt shaker a shake   *(Hand extended to center; shake.)*
   And pop myself about.   *(Hop around self in a small circle.)*

2. Chorus (Here we go...)
   I put my butter in,   *(Hand movement as above.)*
   I put my butter out.   *(Hand movement as above.)*
   I give my butter a pour,   *(Hand movement; pour motion.)*
   And pop myself about.

3. Chorus
   I put my bowl in,   *(One hop step towards center.)*
   I put my bowl out.   *(One hop step away from center.)*
   Give my bowl a treat   *(Pantomime filling bowl with popcorn.)*
   And pop myself about!

54

Recipes
Precious Popcorn Treats

8 cups popped popcorn   1 (24 oz) pkg. miniature marshmallows
½ cup margarine   1 (1 lb.) can salted cocktail peanuts
1 (10 oz) pkg. small gum drop candies

1. Melt butter over low heat in large saucepan.
2. Add marshmallows; stir until melted.
3. Combine popcorn, peanuts, and gumdrops in a large bowl.
4. Pour marshmallow sauce over popcorn mixture; mix well.
5. Press popcorn into well-greased rectangular 9" x 13" cake pan.
6. Cool until firm. Cut into squares. (Number of squares will vary according to cutting pattern used.)

Native American Popcorn Soup

½ gallon milk
1 quart half and half
2 (15.5 oz) cans regular corn
2 cups crushed soda crackers
4 cups popped popcorn   1 teaspoon nutmeg   ½ teaspoon pepper

Place all ingredients in a slow cooker; blend well. Heat until soup is hot. Spoon into small cups or bowls and top with a few extra popcorn flakes. Makes approximately 40 ½ cup servings.

Kookie Karamel Korn

7 quarts popped popcorn   2 cups brown sugar
  (about 1 ½ cups unpopped)   ½ teaspoon cream of tartar
2 cups dry roasted peanuts   ½ cup light corn syrup
1 cup margarine   1 teaspoon baking soda

Use 2 cups of one, or combination of all: raisins, chocolate chips, multi-colored sprinkles, mini-cinnamon candies, dried fruit chunks, gumdrops, nuts

Placed popped corn in large roasting pan. Pour peanuts over popcorn; set aside. In large pan, boil margarine, brown sugar, cream of tartar, and corn syrup for five minutes; stir occasionally. Remove from heat; add baking soda and blend well. Pour over popcorn and peanuts; combine. Place in pre-heated 250° F oven for one hour, stirring every 15 minutes. Remove and pour popcorn mixture onto wax paper; spread out popcorn mixture. Sprinkle with 2 Kookie cups; press gently to make kookie additions stick. Cool completely. Store Kookie Karamel Korn in self-sealing bags or jars with tight lids.

Popcorn Games
Old Maid

Choose one student to be "it" and ask that student to stand in the middle of the room with eyes closed. The rest of the class pretends to be popcorn kernels about to pop and crouches down low to the floor. The teacher (or a designated student) silently taps one crouching student on the shoulder (who will be the Old Maid). When "it" says, "Old Maid, Old Maid, where can you be?" all crouching students begin to hop around, except for the tapped student. He/She hides somewhere in the room or just outside the classroom door. After a few moments, "it" says, "Old Maid, Old Maid, let me see!" Everyone stops hopping and stays crouched down. "It" opens his/her eyes and tries to guess who the Old Maid (unpopped kernel) is. If "it" guesses correctly, he/she may have another turn, or choose a new person to be "it". If incorrect, the Old Maid becomes "it".

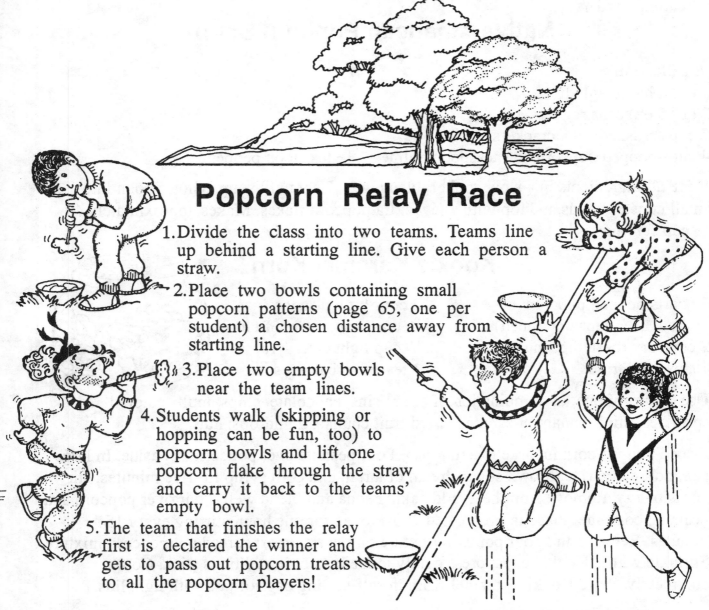

Popcorn Relay Race

1. Divide the class into two teams. Teams line up behind a starting line. Give each person a straw.

2. Place two bowls containing small popcorn patterns (page 65, one per student) a chosen distance away from starting line.

3. Place two empty bowls near the team lines.

4. Students walk (skipping or hopping can be fun, too) to popcorn bowls and lift one popcorn flake through the straw and carry it back to the teams' empty bowl.

5. The team that finishes the relay first is declared the winner and gets to pass out popcorn treats to all the popcorn players!

Homework Reminder Slips

IT'S BEAR-Y ESSENTIAL . . .

that we pop these kernels together tonight!

Then, on the back write:

WHEN we popped the kernels.
WHERE we popped the kernels.
HOW we popped the kernels.
WHO helped pop the kernels.
WHAT did we do while we ate the popped kernels.

Guess What We Are Going To Do . . .

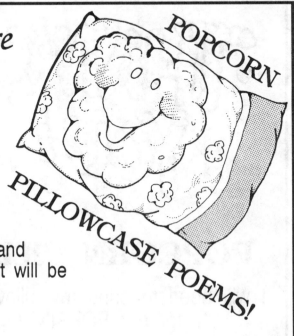

Could you please send a clean, non-printed pillowcase with me to school tomorrow?

I will write and illustrate my poem and then begin to memorize it. I know it will be poppin' terrific fun! Thank you!

Homework Reminder Slips (cont.)

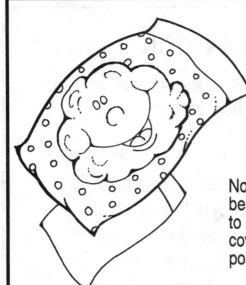

Wow!
Doesn't my
POPCORN PILLOWCASE
POEM
look poppin' great?

Now it is time for me to memorize my poem. The best way is to let me "sleep" on it! Before I go to bed, listen to me say/read my poem (which is covering my pillow) and then I can have sweet popcorn dreams!

For helping me
memorize my

POPCORN PILLOWCASE POEM!

I will need to bring my pillowcase back to school tomorrow for our POPPIN' GOOD PERFORMANCE!

Culminating Activities

Before A Poppin' Good Performance begins, allow time for evaluation of skills and/or concepts presented. Some suggested evaluation strategies are:

> Individual Popcorn Pass-Around Sheet (Modification of # 1, page 6)
> Popcorn Facts Web (Modification of # 3, page 6)
> Is That a Fact! Journal Writings (# 6, page 18)
> Student-Driven Products (Books/Projects Class or Individually created)
> Formal Test-Taking (Spelling Test, Worksheets)

A Poppin' Good Performance!

Invite faculty, staff, another class, and/or families to your class performance (see Day VI, page 15) to share in the learning that has taken place during this thematic unit. Allow the students to act as hosts and hostesses before the performance begins by showing the guests the pop-rific student-authored products displayed around the room and in the hallway. This culminating activity has four objectives that are interwoven into the performance. Foster student ownership in the performance by allowing students to choose what activity will be presented during each performance segment. Here are some suggestions which match the objective for each performance segment. Use the box as a management tool. If students select that activity, put a small pencil mark in that space.

Segment One: Students will effectively communicate through an oral presentation.

- ☐ Perform Quotation Popcorn Play (# 2, page 9)

- ☐ Share Book Jacket Illustrations (page 34)

- ☐ Sing Popcorn Songs (page 54)

- ☐ Present Results From Science Experiments (pages 45, 47, 48)

- ☐ Introduce the Author Tomie dePaola (page 23)

Culminating Activities *(cont.)*

Segment Two: Students will demonstrate understanding of the thematic unit topics.

☐ Discuss Popcorn Plant Facts (page 69)

☐ Share Kernel Knowledge (page 70)

☐ Present Corn-y People Research Reports (# 3, page 19)

☐ Read/Discuss Native American Corn Cycle Fold-Out Books (# 4, page 20)

☐ Read Excerpts From Is That a Fact! Journals (# 6, page 18)

Segment Three: Students will read written text/print.

Students read...

☐ The Best Thing About _____ Is... (# 1, page 18)

☐ Popcorn Pillowcase Poems (page 42)

☐ *Popcorn* By Frank Asch

☐ Popcorn Popping Myths (# 3, page 17)

☐ Pop-Open Dragon Books (# 1, page 26)

Segment Four: Students will display cooperative learning skills.

☐ Present the Popcorn Dragon Stick Puppet Play (# 1, page 25)

☐ Show/Discuss Poppin' Polite Corn Field Sayings (# 3, page 26)

☐ Discuss Working Together During Math Activities (pages 43-44)

☐ Share "Our Popcorn Book" For Mr. dePaola (# 5, page 20)

☐ Pass Out Popcorn Food Treat Students Have Prepared (page 55)

☐ Teacher Passes Out an Award to Each Student With a Positive Comment on How He/She Cooperates With the Other Students (page 79)

When The Performance is Over...

When the guests have left, allow your students to have their own closure activity by enjoying a fun-filled Popcorn Shower!

1. Put a clean sheet down on the floor.
2. Place a hot air popper in the middle, removing the lid.
3. Add kernels; turn on. Students sit around edge of sheet with paper cups.
4. When popcorn flakes pop out, students try to catch them with their cups.

Important Note: This should only be attempted with adult supervision.

Look What's Popping!
Bulletin Board

Objectives

This bulletin board has been designed as a tool to help reinforce skills taught/reviewed, as well as to display student-made products (writing samples, art, math equations).

Materials

Butcher paper or fabric (for background); colored construction paper (for bulletin board pieces); black marker (for outlining and face details); scissors; staples or pushpins

Construction

1. Reproduce pattern pieces for popcorn box and large and/or small popcorn pieces (dependent on use of bulletin board display) onto colored construction paper; cut out.

2. With the black marker, add details to box and popcorn.

3. Staple/Pin background into place. Add box and appropriate popcorn pieces. Add title.

Bulletin Board Activities

1. For displaying student-made products, place only the popcorn box and title onto the background. Each day, as students complete various work, display on the bulletin board. (Be sure to eventually include a sample of everyone's work.)

2. Create as displayed below:

Prior to lesson: Draw (or cut and paste) several sets of before/after pictures onto small popcorn pattern pieces. Place pieces in the popcorn box. Have students observe popcorn kernels (before heat). Pop the kernels. Observe (and taste!) the delicious after heat results. Pull out the first pair of prepared before/after popcorn cards. Have students classify into correct before/after popcorn pouches; continue with remaining popcorn pieces. To extend activity, provide each student with two blank small popcorn pieces and allow them to illustrate their own creative before/after popcorn cards to add to bulletin board display!

3. Place spelling/language/math/science/social studies words on small popcorn pieces and have words "popping" out of the box for introduction and/or review purposes.

Bulletin Board *(cont.)*

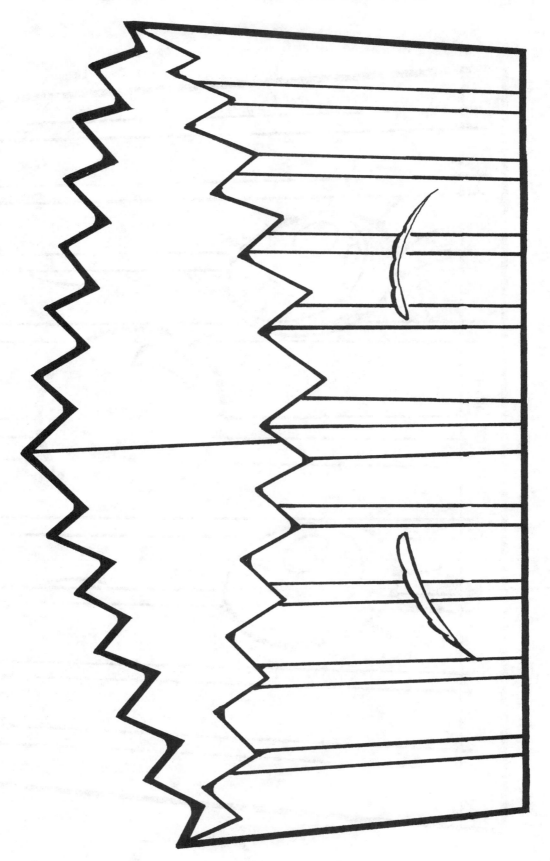

Bulletin Board *(cont.)*

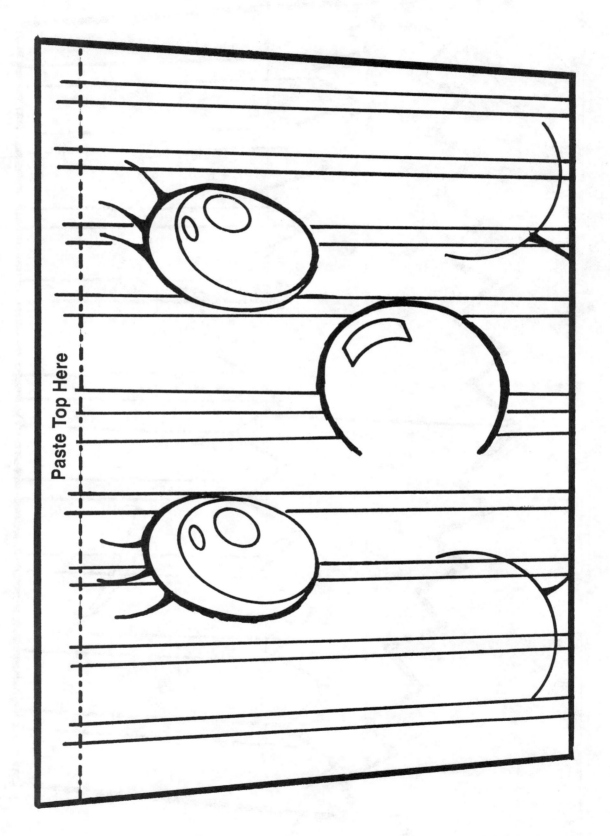

Bulletin Board *(cont.)*

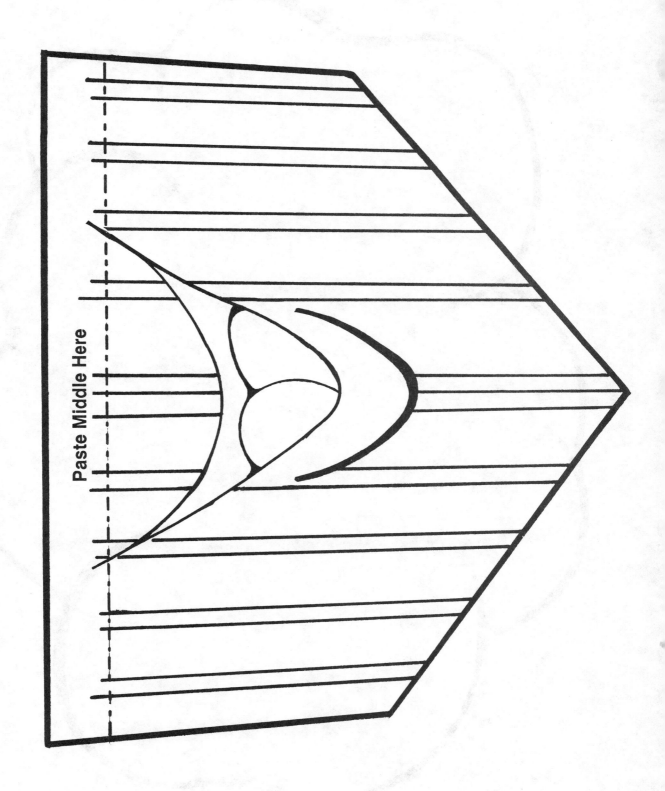

Paste Middle Here

Bulletin Board *(cont.)*

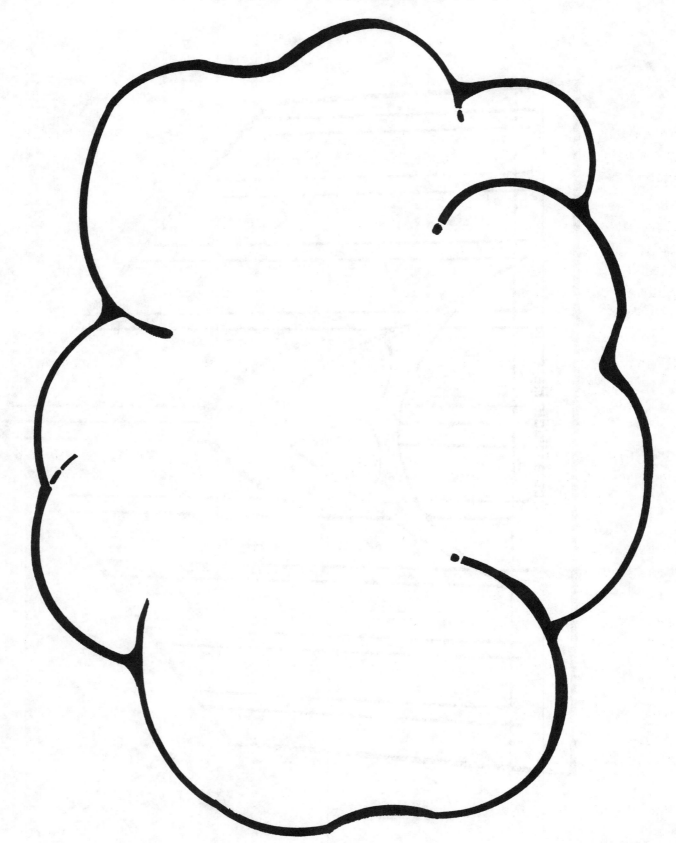

Watch Your Language, Please!

Types of Corn

There are seven present-day varieties of corn. They are defined below and illustrated on page 68.

dent corn: (cow corn, field corn) Each kernel has a small dent in it, hence the name. This is not very tasty to humans, but animals love it. Most farmers feed their livestock this variety of corn.

flint corn: (ornamental, Indian corn) This corn's beautiful red, black, blue, yellow, and white kernels make pretty fall harvest and Thanksgiving displays. The kernels are very hard and do not taste good, so flint corn is used mainly for ornamental displays. The Pilgrims did raise flint corn, cross-pollinating it with dent corn, to create an edible variety.

flour corn: This corn contains very soft kernels, due to a low-starch content. Because of this, flour corn can easily be crushed into corn flour (masa) and used for cooking purposes.

pod corn: This corn is pretty to look at, but awful to eat! This variety of corn is unique because each kernel is wrapped in a separate husk. It is used exclusively for flower arrangements and ornamental decorating.

popcorn: The only variety of corn that can be popped by heat to form a tasty, edible food item. (It is not dried sweet corn!)

sweet corn: (corn-on-the-cob, table corn) This corn is the type we enjoy eating. Its sweetness is due to a high sugar and starch content. Early Native Americans did not have this variety of corn to eat. They mainly ate dent or flint corn.

waxy corn: This corn was named for its wax-like appearance due to high-starch content. It is used mainly as a thickening agent in such products as instant pudding mixes, gravies and sauces, glues, and baby powders.

wild corn: Wild corn is now extinct, but was the "ancestor" of today's corn family. The small ears of corn found in the Bat Cave in New Mexico (over 5,600 years old!) are thought to be this type.

Types of Corn *(cont.)*

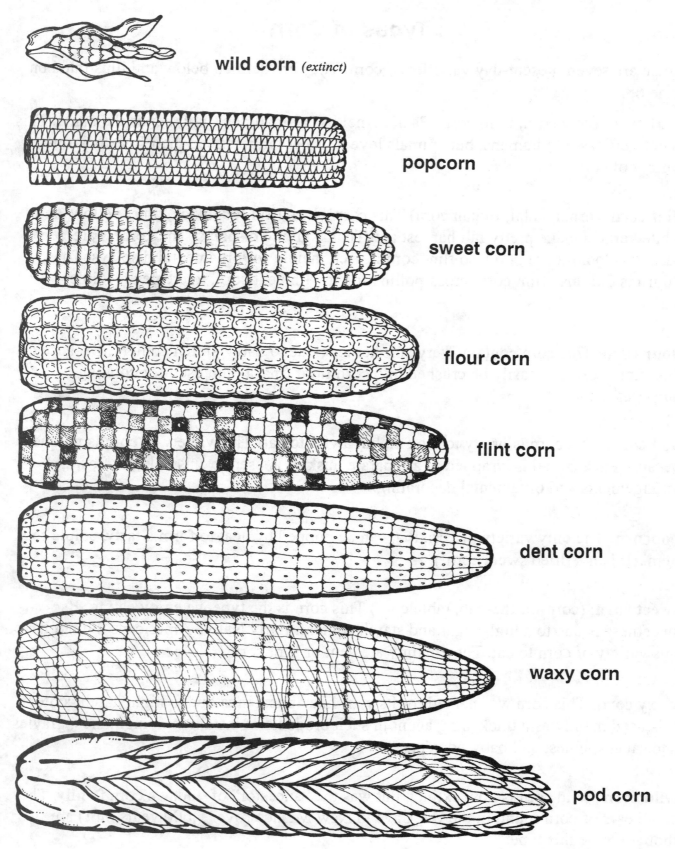

wild corn *(extinct)*

popcorn

sweet corn

flour corn

flint corn

dent corn

waxy corn

pod corn

      68

The Popcorn Plant

corn: Corn belongs to the grass family of plants. Corn stalks contain a soft, spongy tissue rich in sugar and starch. It is believed that corn originated in South or Central America.

ear: The seed-bearing spike of the corn plant. Each ear contains cluster (rows) of female flowers called silk.

husk: The dry outer covering around the ear which protects the silk and kernels.

leaves: The leaves grow out from the nodes. Veins run lengthwise through the leaves which make the edges look wavy.

nodes: (joints) Nodes separate the stalk into sections. These joints help make the plant stronger.

prop roots: Extra above-ground roots to help "prop up" tall corn plants.

silk: The female flower located in the ear. Each strand of silk, when fertilized by the pollen, will form one corn kernel!

tassel: The male flower located at the top of the plant. It sheds pollen which is "caught" by the silk.

Kernel Vocabulary

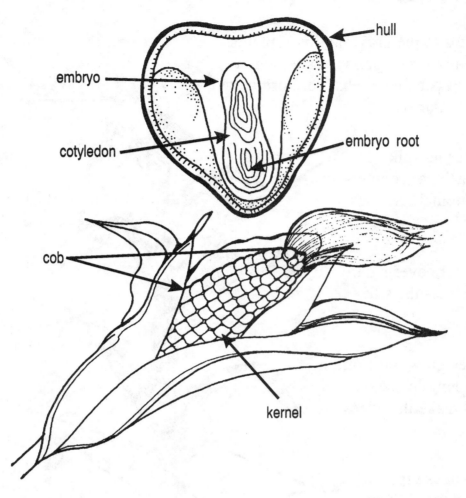

cob: The tough, spike-shaped core on which the corn kernels grow.

cotyledon: The seed leaf which contains starch and protein to provide energy to the budding corn plant.

embryo: The center of the grain seed which becomes the corn plant.

embryo root: Inside of the embryo, the embryo root will become the root system for the corn plant.

endosperm: Energy storage area, containing starch and protein to feed the embryo.

hull: (seed coat) The tough outer covering of the kernel which protects the seed embryo.

hybrid: Man-made varieties of popcorn plants which are created when one type of popcorn plant is fertilized (by hand) with a different type of popcorn plant to create a brand new type of popcorn plant.

kernel: The popcorn seed (technically it is the ovary which surrounds the corn seed).

plumule: The embryo bud that will grow into the corn stem and first corn plant leaves.

Corn-y Terminology

bee wings: When the hull shatters as the popcorn is popping it breaks into tiny bits called bee wings. (Have you ever had a wing stuck in your teeth?)

husking bee: An old-fashioned get-together held in late October where everyone sits around and talks while the picked corn gets husked.

flake: A popped popcorn kernel.

hulless popcorn: Name given to a variety of popcorn which eludes to the popcorn containing no hull, but is untrue. All popcorn has a hull. Hulless is a hybrid popcorn with a thinner hull that mega-shatters, therefore not allowing bee wings to be formed.

husk: *(verb)* The act of removing the husk from the ear of corn.

maize: Native American term for corn which means "our life." Early Native American and South American Indians used corn as the main staple of their diet.

Corn-y Terminology *(cont.)*

mushroom: One of the two shapes of popped popcorn. It is smaller than snowflake, and has a nice round shape. It is used primarily for candied popcorn because it does not crumble easily.

old maids: (widow, duds, flopcorn) The unpopped kernels left after popcorn kernels have been heated and popped.

popcorn: The white puffy mass formed by a popped popcorn kernel (the popped grain).

shuck: The action of pulling off the corn husk from the ear.

snowflake: (butterfly) One of the two shapes of popped popcorn. It is the one sold in most grocery stores and sold at most popcorn-eating events. It pops up very big and is shaped somewhat like a cloud. Because it fluffs up so much, it is the favorite popcorn for theaters and other entertainment events to sell because you can pop less, but get more!

zea mays everta: The scientific name for popcorn (There are over 2,000 varieties!).

Corn-y People

Charlie Cretors

In 1885, Charlie Cretors was busy making peanut roasters. He decided to try something new, popcorn! He invented a small, moveable steam-powered machine that popped popcorn in front of his store. Some people passing by were salesman. They told other store owners about Charlie's popping machine. Other stores wanted one, too. Soon Charlie Cretors spent his time making the all-new automatic popcorn popping machine!

Christopher Columbus

In 1492, Christopher Columbus was sailing to India and got lost. He ended up in the New World, which would later be known as America. He met Native Americans there. As a gift, they gave Columbus popcorn decorations and popcorn seeds. He took this special gift of maize back to his homeland, Spain.

Quadequina

When the Pilgrims invited the Wampanog Native Americans to their first Thanksgiving celebration, they were in for a special treat!

Quadequina, the brother of the Wamanog Chief, Massasoit, brought a gift of popcorn in a small deerskin bag. The Pilgrims called it "Indian Corn."

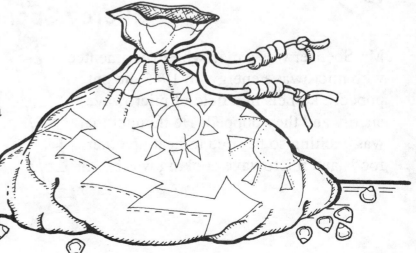

Corn-y People (cont.)

Orville Redenbacher

Mr. Redenbacher has been called the "Popcorn King of the Twentieth Century." Ever since he was young, he has been fascinated with popcorn. He started his own business, The Orville Redenbacher Popcorn Company, and began experimenting with new popcorn hybrids. He created over 30,000 different kinds of new popcorn hybrid plants every year until, finally, in 1965, he created a superior popping corn called "Gourmet Variety Popcorn."

Cloid Smith

Cloid Smith was concerned about popcorn kernels drying out in the popcorn boxes while waiting to be sold on the shelves of grocery stores. In 1924, he took his concern to the American Can Company. Engineers designed a special metal can that kept air out. This can was the ancestor of today's soda pop cans!

Percy Spencer

Mr. Spencer was a man who experimented with microwave energy. In 1945, he put popcorn kernels in a field of microwave energy and they popped! He thought that was exciting so he tried to heat up other foods and microwave cooking was born!

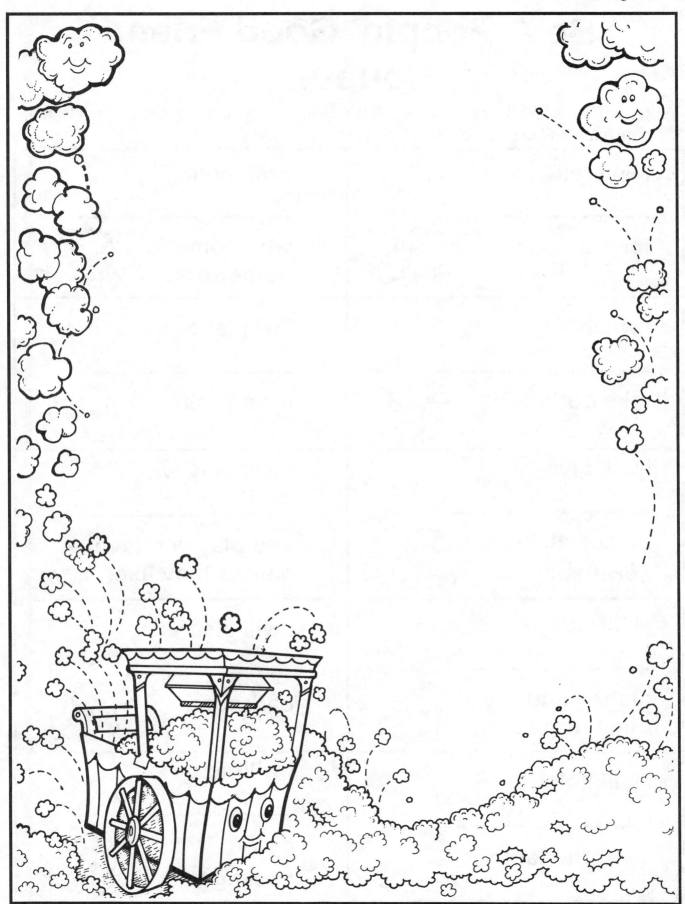

Be A Poppin' Good Friend Coupons

Write a different friend's name on each line (remember, your family can be friends, too).
Color pictures and cut out on lines. Give coupons to your friends!

I will read to _____ *(Name)* **for 1/2 hour.**	**I will help** _____ *(Name)* **with some homework.**
I will help _____ *(Name)* **take out trash.**	**I will take** _____ *(Name)* **for a walk.**
I will give _____ *(Name)* **a special surprise!**	**I will play with** _____ *(Names)* **and play whatever games they like.**
I will wash _____'s *(Name)* **dishes and dry them, too.**	**I will clean** _____'s *(Name)* **bedroom.**
I will help _____ *(Name)* **clear the table.**	**I will help** _____ *(Name)* **carry packages.**

Popcorn Review Cards

1.

What does "maize" mean in the Native American language?

2.

What are the two shapes of popcorn flakes?

3.

What did Charlie Cretors invent?

4.

What was the name of the Native American who gave popcorn to the Pilgrims at the first Thanksgiving feast?

5.

How many pounds of popcorn do Americans eat in one year?

6.

Where is most of the popcorn grown in the United States?

7.

What brings Old Maids back to life?

8.

Why did Native Americans of long ago think popcorn popped?

9.

What are popped popcorn kernels called?

10.

What popcorn variety did Orville Redenbacher create?

Popcorn Review Cards *(cont.)*

11. Should salt be added before or after popcorn is popped?	**12.** What are the three parts of a popcorn plant?
13. Approximately how many kernels are in one cup?	**14.** What are bee wings?
15. Where were the oldest popcorn kernels found?	**16.** What are the names of the seven varieties popcorn?
17. What makes a popcorn kernel pop?	**18.** What does hulless popcorn mean?
19. What story about popcorn did Tomie dePaola write?	**20.** Why should popcorn kernels be kept in the refrigerator?

78

Awards

This may sound a bit

CORNY

but I think you're the best!

_____
Name

_____   _____
Teacher   **Date**

You did a . . .

POPPIN' GREAT
JOB!

_____
Name

_____   _____
Teacher   Date

Bibliography

Core Books

Asch, Frank. *Popcorn*. Parents' Magazine Press, 1979.
de Paola, Tomie. *The Popcorn Book*. Scholastic Books, 1978.
Thayer, Jane. *The Popcorn Dragon*. Morrow Junior Books, 1953.

Nonfiction Books

Aliki. *Corn is Maize, The Gifts of the Indians*. Harper Trophy, 1976
Selsman, Millicent. *Popcorn*. Morrow, 1976.
Woodside, Dave. *What Makes Popcorn Pop?* Atheneum, 1980.
Wyler, Rose. *Science Fun with Peanuts and Popcorn*. Messner, 1986.

Books by Frank Asch

Bear Shadow. Simon and Schuster, 1988
Bear's Bargain. Simon and Schuster, 1989
Happy Birthday Moon. Simon and Schuster, 1988
Oats and Wild Apples. Holiday, 1988
Sand Cake. Crown, 1987

Books by Tomie de Paola

Bill and Pete. Putnam, 1978.
Charlie Needs a Cloak. Prentice-Hall, 1973.
The Legend of the Old Befana. Harcourt, 1980.
Nana Upstairs, Nana Downstairs. Putnam, 1973.
Watch Out for the Chicken Feet in Your Soup. Prentice-Hall, 1974.

Books by Jane Thayer

Gus Was a Real Dumb Ghost. Morrow, 1982
The Puppy Who Wanted a Boy. Morrow, 1986
Quiet on Account of a Dinosaur. Morrow, 1988

Address

The Popcorn Institute
401 North Michigan
Chicago, IL 60611-4267
(312) 644-6610

Page 50

Answers

The First Thanksgiving

Page 77 and 78
1. Our Life
2. Snowflake and Mushroom
3. Popcorn Popping Machine
4. Quadequina
5. Over 500 Million Pounds
6. Midwest United States
7. Soak In A Little Bit Of Water
8. A Little Demon Got Angry
9. Flakes
10. Gourmet Variety Popcorn
11. Depends On Results (page 47)
12. Ear, Husk, Leaves, Nodes, Silk, Tassel, Prop Roots, Roots
13. Approximately 1,600 Kernels
14. Tiny Bits Of Shattered Hulls
15. Bat Cave, New Mexico, U.S.A.
16. Pop, Sweet, Flour, Flint, Dent, Waxy, Pod
17. Moisture Inside Kernel Turns To Steam
18. Not Much Hull Remains After Kernels Are Popped
19. *The Popcorn Book*
20. Kernels Keep Their Moisture